SELECTED POEMS

Other Books by Denise Levertov

The Double Image

Here and Now

Overland to the Islands

With Eyes at the Back of Our Heads

The Jacob's Ladder

O Taste and See

The Sorrow Dance

Guillevic

Selected
Poems

Translated by

Denise
Levertov

New Directions

Manufactured in the United States of America.

Published simultaneously in Canada by McClelland & Stewart Limited.

New Directions Books are published for James Laughlin
by New Directions Publishing Corporation, 333 Sixth Avenue,
New York 10014.

Contents

1

Guillevic is a Breton, born at Carnac of peasant stock. His poetry has deep roots in that inheritance. The great ritual places of the Celts, whether in Wales or Cornwall, Ireland or Brittany, the places where the great and small stones or *menhirs,* are gathered in powerful and enigmatic testimony to forgotten certainties, are landscapes of a profound austerity. In such landscapes the senses are undistracted from the elemental: rock, sky, sea are there not backgrounds but presences. Beginning in such a place, Guillevic learned to recognize all else in life likewise as *presence,* not as incidental properties. Man, bird, cloud, lake, night, death, the sunlight—he knows them as Powers and Principalities, meets them face to face, and disdains the folly of attempting to use them as mere autobiographical adornments. This atheist is a radically religious poet.

His indignation at the use and misuse of some human beings by others, at the depersonalization of men by industrial and military interests, takes its force from the same source, that recognition of irreducible *presence* in all creation, animate and inanimate; but he is also a Marxist and a professional economist, and his moral indignation is accompanied by a cold and clear understanding of historical process.

The scrupulous simplicity of his diction often reminds me of that of Antonio Machado. (Guillevic does not read Spanish and does not know Machado's work.) Like Machado's, the shortest and seemingly plainest poems of Guillevic are often the most difficult to translate. In such short poems of Machado, the play of sound is essential, and the translator, without room to maneuver, is left with a flat literal.

> Entre el vivir y el soñar
> hay una tercera cosa.
> Adivínala.

The music, the dense weave in small compass, of the a's and r's, is absent in English:

> Between living and dreaming
> is a third thing.
> Guess it.

In longer poems the translator can often find possibilities for assonantial interplay between other words of the total structure than those in which such interplay exists in the original, and so may construct equivalents—not reproductions—of the music he has heard. In short poems there is rarely that opportunity, unless the translator is willing to depart radically from the images of the original.

Again like Machado, Guillevic avoids the easily opulent image, the blurred emotive impression. He trusts the hard, the plain, the stripped, to speak for itself. He refuses to say more than he feels.

> Prenez un toit de vieilles tuiles
> Un peu après midi.
>
> Placez tout à côté
> Un tilleul déjà grand
> Remué par le vent,
> . . .
> Laissez-les faire.
> Regardez-les.
>
> ("Recipe")

But his feeling, his passion for life ("Ma folie/ est de ce monde"), his passionate awareness of death, everywhere inseparable from life, his sharp and sensuous eye and ear are complex. And so the simplicity of diction, the plain and hard naming of things without descriptive qualification, reverberates, in the highly charged condensation of Guillevic's poems, with the ambiguity, the unfathomable mystery, of natural objects. To enter his work is to enter a kind of verbal Carnac, a gathering of sacred stones.

2

Eugène Guillevic was born at Carnac in 1907. His father had been a sailor, but after 1909 became a *gendarme*. His mother worked as a seamstress. When Guillevic was two years old his father was assigned to an industrial town on the Belgian frontier, where the family lived in a police barracks. When he was five they returned to Brittany, to the village of Saint-Jean-Brévelay, about forty kilometers from Carnac. He used to spend his holidays at Carnac with an aunt who was a laundress. Jean Tortel writes of this landscape, "A country of scattered hamlets, surrounded by heaths that have today been reclaimed but then were wild, rising in bare hills, with pinetrees growing here and there. Windmills. Much wind, many birds." At Saint-Jean-Brévelay too the Guillevics lived in a bleak barracks. His father was mobilized in 1914. Life was hard and poor. In 1919 they moved again, this time to Ferrette in Alsace, close to the Swiss border—a softer, gentler, landscape. Here Guillevic spent his adolescence, learned Alsatian and German, read Hugo and La Fontaine in school, discovered Lamartine, who was perhaps the first poet to awaken his enthusiasm for poetry, Rousseau, and—through an Alsatian poet, Nathan Katz, with whom he struck up a friendship—the German 19th-century poets and later, Rilke. At home no one read books; but somehow it was not long before Guillevic laid his hands on Verlaine, Baudelaire, Rimbaud. At nineteen he left Ferrette and did his military service at Besançon and Mayence. Soon after, another Alsatian poet gave him the poems of Trakl; and Trakl has remained for him one of the most intimately important of poets, along with Hölderlin whose work he did not come to know until some ten years later. It is curious to note that, outside of school, Guillevic did not hear French spoken around him, but, in early childhood, Breton, and in adolescence, Alsatian, until he was nearly twenty. Jean Tortel, in that same essay to which I am indebted for most of these facts (a critical and biographical introduction to the "Poètes d'aujourd'hui" edition of Guillevic's selected poems, 1963), speculates on the possible influence on his work of this early detachment from the language in which he writes; perhaps, he suggests, it helped to form "the consideration with which he approaches words, the space he leaves between them and himself. For him each vocable (plate, chair, nightingale) is not something taken for granted, something everyday." One might say, indeed, that his relation to words is truly phenomenological—and I think here of the poetic phenomenology of Gaston Bachelard, that great man whom Guillevic knew and revered.

Like Francis Ponge—and like, in a very different manner, Rilke—Guillevic has many poems devoted to *things;* in this selection, "A Hammer" and "A Nail" are obvious examples, or, in a deeper vein, "The Rocks," and "Gulls." His relation to *the thing* is, however, less objective than Ponge's (as Tortel notes, defining the tone of Ponge's *Le Parti pris des choses* as often being that of a lesson given by the object) and less self-identifying, or empathic, than Rilke's. Guillevic regards the primordial object with a kind of terror; it seems sometimes that he names it, as has been said by Léon-Gabriel Gros, to exorcize it—rather than either to reveal it or to extend his own life by identifying with it. Yet that passion for the world (and "there is no other world/ in which to rest" he says) of which I have spoken, subsumes that terror, that recurring sense of the malignity of nature, makes it an element of passion, an awe-full means of adoration. And the sense of nature's malignity alternates, or coexists, with his humane grief and anger at man's inhumanity to man:

> Et puis, nous ne sommes pas malades
> De la terre.

> L'ennemi,
> Nous le connaissons.

His Communism, and perhaps the poverty of his own youth, sometimes seem to make him divide mankind rather too sharply into the oppressors (see "Big Business") and the oppressed (see "Portrait"). However, anyone who supposes an avowed Communist will write only social-realist or propagandistic poetry will find themselves confuted by the ambiguity and even mysticism of Guillevic's writing. When I said to him that he was a religious poet he replied, "Of course. But mine is a religion of earth, not of heaven."

There seems to have been a crisis in his development in the middle 1950's, when *31 Sonnets* appeared, with a preface by Aragon. These are by no means his only "political" or overtly "engaged" poems (*Exécutoire*, 1947, and *Gagner*, 1949, in particular, contain many), but in these he seems—in the adoption of the sonnet form itself, as if to give to the common reader an absolutely familiar point of entry—to have been making a deliberate effort to write a kind of poem he felt (or had by external pressures, from the intellectual milieu in which he at that time found himself, been made to feel) he *ought* to be writing: which he owed to the social struggle. A number of the sonnets—including the one I have included here, "Native Land"—seem to me admirable works in their way. But Guillevic himself seems to have felt it was not *his* way, for after a lapse of five years the next work he published was *Carnac*, a major sequence in which he reverted to, and further refined, the distinctive voice, the condensed and usually unrhymed forms, that characterized his earlier volumes and which he had continued to develop in his books of the last seven years.

I have spoken of the affinity I feel exists, unknown to Guillevic, between his work and some, at least, of Antonio Machado's. Even more notable, I believe, are the parallels between Guillevic and William Carlos Williams. No doubt, loving Williams as I do, and important for me as he has been, it was some sense of this likeness that first drew me to Guillevic—who, again, does not yet read enough English to read Williams. Opening a volume of Williams at random to find examples to cite, I come at once upon "Lament" (*Collected Later Poems,* page 76) and "A History of Love" (page 77). "Lament" begins:

> What face, in the water,
> distinct
> yet washed by obscurity?
>
> The willow supplants its own
> struggling rafters
> (of winter branches)
>
> by a green radiance. Is it
> old or young?
> But what this face
>
> reflected beyond the bare structures
> of a face
> shining from the creaseless
>
> water . . .

And "A History of Love" begins:

> And would you gather turds
> for your grandmother's garden?
> Out with you, then, dustpan and broom;
> she has seen the horse passing!
>
> Out you go, bold again
> as you promise always to be.
> Stick out your tongue at the neighbors
> that her flowers may grow.

There is in either of these, different from each other

though they are, a note, a feeling-tone, I find also in Guillevic; and had I not, in order not to seem to force a point, deliberately chosen at random, I could provide even closer, or more obvious, parallels—though it is the Williams of the *Earlier* and *Later Collected Poems,* and some of the very last short poems, not the Williams of *Paterson* and *The Desert Music* and the other longer late poems that Guillevic seems to me to resemble. Guillevic's poems have tended, on the whole, to get shorter (though often these short poems form long sequences) while Williams, not only in the epic *Paterson* but in *The Desert Music,* in "Asphodel, That Greeny Flower" and in the grandeur of other late poems, expanded his forms. In *Carnac* Guillevic has created a sustained and profound booklength poem, but formally his method in it remains the sequence of short poems, each paradoxically autonomous yet closely related to one another. It is in respect for this vital interrelationship of its parts to the whole that I have not attempted to include any excerpts from *Carnac.*

3

My interest as a translator is not in providing *reproductions* but in *reconstituting* the original in such English as I imagine the poet might have used if he wrote in English. That is why I would never attempt to translate the work of a poet with whom I did not, myself, feel a good deal of affinity; nor individual poems that I could not at all imagine myself to have written. I would never deliberately pad out a line in order to reproduce a rhythmic structure; on the other hand, a more or less literal version will sometimes, in the new language, seem less concise than the original, and by dropping a few words one may get an effect more genuinely accurate. As an example of how I have approached this problem, here is the first literal draft of "The Task" which the reader may compare with the final translation on page 137:

Overture / or Opening

When each of your days
becomes holy to you,

when each of your hours
becomes holy to you,

when each of your moments
becomes holy to you,

when the earth and you,
space and you,
shall carry the holy
throughout your days

then you will be
in the fields of glory.

This was the first Guillevic poem I ever read, and it seemed and still seems a most marvelous poem in French; but I have no doubt in my own mind that *in English* it is *more like itself* in my pruned version than in the superficially "faithful" one. It will be noted that I have taken the liberty of retitling it, in a way that *in English* sounds to me more meaningful than any way I could think of translating the word *"ouverture."*

"Beyond a certain point one cannot reconcile the demands of translation and of poetry, and must opt for one or the other," says A. C. Graham in the fascinating introduction to his *Poems of the Late T'ang* (Penguin). "Partial reconciliation is possible because at least one element in poetry, imagery, can function effectively in another language. But however much the imagery may vitalize the rhythm and diction of the English, it is still true that the translator is trying to force into one language an imaginative process natural to another. The result may, and ought to be, poetry—we shall not argue over definitions—but it will not give us the final satisfaction of making its impression by the perfect, the only adequate, arrangement of words. . . . Every poetic translator must therefore decide whether to stop at the point from which the English reader will have the best view of Omar Khayyam, or attempt the further step by which Edward Fitzgerald takes his place in the line of English poets."

I am not fully satisfied, by any means, with most of my versions of Guillevic; but A. C. Graham's definition of the translator's choices does describe my intention, which has been to render these poems in such a way that they would seem, in English, to be written in the language of poetry and not in Translationese.

I have included no poem that, no matter how I pored over it with Larousse and two French-English dictionaries, I could not feel sure I understood properly; nevertheless, I have often felt presumptuous at having undertaken the task of presenting Guillevic to an American public that scarcely knows his name; and have taken courage again only when a poem has seemed, at any rate, to *work* as an English (or American) poem, even if to a bilingual reader it must fall short as a representation of the original. But after all, translations are not *for* truly bilingual readers. I am indebted to Mr. George Quasha and to M. Daniel Mauroc for the correction of some actual misunderstandings. I have never intentionally changed an image (with one exception, noted on page 11—"I had married a wand of willow . . ."). Therefore I believe I can call these versions *translations,* not *imitations,* as I would if I had embroidered on Guillevic's themes. In any case where I have added a word it will have been for the sake of clarity—that is, of saying in English what it has seemed to me Guillevic meant, and which seemed to take more words in English than clarity demanded in French.

D. L.

Cela agace beaucoup de gens que les poètes se croient, se disent découvreurs du vrai, porteurs de la loi nouvelle, voyants. Pourquoi eux? Quelle Providence les a investis? Qui les a sacrés? Il est temps de désacraliser le poète, disent-ils. Essayons d'y voir un peu clair:

Le poète est homme puisqu'il est un homme. Et donc, il est comme tous les autres hommes, comme tout le monde. C'est évident—et ce n'est pas tout à fait vrai.

Car le poète est celui qui a le pouvoir de faire avec la langue de son pays certaines combinaisons dont les autres hommes ont besoin pour se trouver, trouver le monde—pour vivre.

D'où lui vient ce pouvoir singulier? Mystère sans doute. Mais, assurément, il n'aurait pas ce pouvoir s'il n'était pas doué d'une grande sensibilité à l'égard de tout ce qui constitue sa langue nationale: aux mots, à la syntaxe, aux usages.

C'est à cause de cette sensibilité qu'il peut, avec les élèments de sa langue, faire un langage, ce langage qui lui permettra d'en dire plus que les élèments de la langue et leurs combinaisons ne consentent généralement à dire.

Une telle sensibilité ne va pas sans une égale sensibilité aux choses autres que le langage. Le poète est un homme d'une sensibilité de fleur et de feuille à tout ce qui fait le monde extérieur et intérieur. Je crois que c'est cette sensibilité qui lui permet les rapports qu'il a avec le langage; c'est elle qui l'oblige à ces rapports.

Cette explication est-elle suffisante? Montre-t-elle pourquoi le poète est un homme chez qui l'exigence de bonheur pour lui et pour les autres est si forte? Montre-t-elle pourquoi, au dire des poètes, nous vivons comme dans la doublure de la vie?

Pour les poètes, il y a du chemin à faire pour arriver à vivre du vrai côté de la vie, dans sa face enfin avouable, celle qui ne se voit jusqu'ici que dans les moments excep-

It troubles many people that poets believe themselves, speak of themselves as discoverers of what is new, bearers of the new law, seers. Why them? What Providence has so invested them? Who has consecrated them? It is time to deconsecrate the poet, they say. Let us try to see this matter a little more clearly:

The poet is man since he is a man. And thus he is like all other men, like everybody. That is obvious—and it is not quite true.

For the poet is he who has the power to make with the language of his country certain combinations which other men need in order to find themselves, to find the world—to live.

Where does this peculiar power come from? That is without doubt a mystery. But assuredly he would not have this power if he were not endowed with a great sensibility in regard to all that constitutes his native language: to words, syntax, usage.

It is because of this sensibility that the poet can, out of the elements of the existing language, *make* a language, one which will permit him to say more than those elements and their combinations will ordinarily consent to say.

Such a sensibility does not operate without an equal sensibility towards things other than language. The poet is a man with, root and branch, a responsiveness to all that makes up the world, outer and inner. I believe it is this that gives him that rapport he has with language; it necessitates such a rapport.

Is this a sufficient explanation? Does it show why the poet is a man for whom the exigence of happiness for himself and for others is so great? Does it show why, in the speech of poets, we seem to live double the amount of life?

For poets, there is a road that must be travelled in order to arrive at living on the true side of life, that side of it one

tionnels et, en particulier, pendant l'écriture et la lecture du poème.

Je croirais volontiers que cette interrogation du poète à la vie est liée à ses rapports avec le langage, car son matériau, la langue de son pays, est tissé à travers les siècles comme à l'envers de la vie, avec les besoins, les aspirations, les rêves, les certitudes des hommes. C'est dans leur langue que les hommes rêvent à ce que devrait être leur vie. La langue est le confessionnal du peuple.

C'est pourquoi le poète peut parler, lui qui, plus que personne, a droit d'accés au confessional.

Le poète est voyant parce qu'il écoute, là où les autres parlent, ont parlé. Dans la mesure où il sait écouter, il peut parler pour tous, annoncer.

Et il va de soi que, lorsque je dis ici: poète, je ne désigne pas le faiseur de vers, mais cet homme qui écrit un langage torturé où les autres hommes—et la langue elle-même—se reconnais sent pour vrais.

De nos jours prose et poèsie ont la nostalgie de noces qui se renouvellent, aux confins de la parole et du silence.

GUILLEVIC
1968

4

can finally affirm, that side of it that so far is seen only in exceptional moments and in particular during the reading or writing of a poem.

I am willing to believe that the poet's interrogation of life is linked with his rapport with language, for his raw material, the language of his country, has been woven across the centuries as if on the under side of life, out of the needs, the aspirations, the dreams and the certitudes of men. It is in their language that men dream of what their lives ought to be. The language is the confessional of the people.

That is why the poet can speak, he who, more than anyone, has rights of access to that confessional.

The poet is a seer because he listens, where others speak, have spoken. In the measure that he knows how to listen, he is able to speak for all, to foretell.

And it follows from this that, when I say here, poet, I do not mean versifier, but that man who writes a tortured language in which other men—and the language itself—can recognize themselves as true.

In our time prose and poetry long for a renewed marriage, at the borders of the word and of silence.

Il s'agit de voir
Tellement plus clair,

De faire avec les choses
Comme la lumière.

Dans la Grotte aux Glaçons

Dans la grotte aux glaçons
Où la lumière eut peur,

C'est là pendant des mois
Que nous avons été,
Sous les glaçons.

Mais ce n'est qu'une image
Et besoin d'une image,

Car nous étions tapis
dans un lieu sans figure,

Bien au-dessous de la parole.

It's a question of seeing
so much clearer,

of doing to things
what light does to them.

In the Cave of Ice

In the cave of ice
where light was fearful

we have been dwelling
these months,
under the icicles.

But this is only
an image; need for an image;

for where we crouched, hiding,
was an amorphous place

far down below language.

Parlant à la poupée
Dont les yeux rappelaient
Ceux qu'il ne trouvait pas

Et dont les bras tendus
Avaient été cassés
Par lui, un autre soir.

Talking to the doll
whose eyes recalled
those eyes he could not find,

and whose outstretched arms
had been broken
by him, another night.

à Colomba

J'avais épousé la branche du saule
Et bien entendu la plus mal venue.

Nous n'avons pas faits de ces longs voyages
A travers nuages
Vers un fond du ciel.

Mais je suis resté
Pendant des instants ou l'éternité
Comme l'eau dans l'eau.

—Et c'est maintenant qu'il faudrait savoir
Qui, sur le bord de la rivière,
Toucha son épouse,
La branche du saule.

Si c'est encore celui qui souffre tellement
Dans tellement de paysages.

I had married a wand of willow
and so there came to me sorrow.[1]

We never took those long voyages
through clouds towards
a depth of sky.

But I was poised
for moments or for eternity
like water in water.

—And now the time comes when he must know
who, on the riverbank, has touched
his bride,
the willowbranch:

whether it is again he who suffers
so much, and in so many landscapes.

[1] I have departed radically from the literal meaning of the second
line, which is: "and of course the worst one that came along." (D.L.)

à Louis Aragon

La scie va dans le bois,
Le bois est séparé

Et c'est la scie
Qui a crié.

★

La petite truite,
Grosse comme un canif,

Ne trouve plus sa pierre
Dans le grand ruisseau.

★

Tous les crustacés
Qui ont tant de noms

Et bien plus encore
De couleurs, de formes,

Ils ne savent pas
Qu'il y a la mer.

The saw goes into the wood,
the wood splits,

and it's the saw
that screams.

★

The little trout
slim[1] as a penknife

can't find its rock
in the great brook.

★

All the crustaceans
who have so many names

so many forms and
colors,

don't know
there is an ocean.

[1] Literally, "the size of." (D.L.)

★

Ce qui ressemblait à la bien-aimée
C'était la tige des blés tant pressés de mûrir
Quand le soleil pensait déjà à s'incliner.

★

Caressant les arbustes
Au niveau de leur greffe
Dont ils ne souffrent plus qu'en rêve.

★

That which resembled the well-belovèd
was the standing wheat in such haste to ripen,[1]
while the sun was already thinking of going down.

★

Caressing the shrubs
at the point of their graft-scars
where they only hurt now
                    in dreams.

[1] This section might have been more accurately translated if it emphasized the point being made by saying, "What the well-belovèd resembled was a wheat-stalk" etc.: the implication being that the belovèd is young and the lover no longer so. But I like the additional sense here of the lover mistaking, at a distance, the blond wheat for the gleam of her hair and arms. (D.L.)

Il y aura toujours dans l'automne
Une pomme sur le point de tomber.

Il y aura toujours dans l'hiver
Une fontaine sur le point de geler.

Que les corbeaux
S'enfuient de peur à notre approche,
C'est leur droit. Nous pouvons aller.

De l'espoir il y en aura
Sur les rameaux.

Et puis, nous ne sommes pas malades
De la terre.

L'ennemi,
nous le connaissons.

There shall[1] always be, in autumn,
an apple about to drop.

There shall always be, in winter,
a fountain about to freeze.

If the crows
fly in fear at our approach,
it's their right. We can walk on.

There shall be some hope
among the branches.

And besides, it's not from the earth
our sickness comes.

We know
who the enemy is.

[1] I used *shall* rather than *will* for the added sense of formality,
of predictive statement, it gives. (D.L.)

Les bois à Colpo, la mer à Carnac, la lande
A Saint-Jean-Brévelay, j'ai bien vu moi qu'ils ont
Une égale colère et crient sur l'horizon
Par le terrible gris, guéri de la légende,

Qu'ils crient par tous les vents, par les corbeaux en bandes,
Par les couleurs de leurs arbres, de leurs maisons,
Crient contre les maudits et leurs combinaisons
De remettre debout une armée allemande,

Pour nous tenir et s'il faut pour nous tuer
Et voir leur règne encore un peu continuer—
Alors que nous voulons vivre en paix et en joie

Sur la terre autour de nous, belle comme elle est.
La mer à Carnac, les bois à Colpo, qu'ils soient
Entendus, et la lande à Saint-Jean-Brévelay.

16 FÉVRIER 1954

The woods at Colpo, the sea at Carnac, the moor
at Saint-Jean-Brévelay, I have seen that they have
each a profound anger and that they cry out
on the horizon in terrible gray, stripped of legend,

that they cry in the winds, and in the flocks of crows,
and in the color of trees, and in the houses,
cry out against the damned who machinate
to set a German army back on its feet

to hold us down and if need be kill us,
and thereby see their rule still persist—
now when we long to live in peace and joy

upon this earth which is so beautiful.
The sea at Carnac, the woods at Colpo,
may they be heard, and the moor at Brévelay.[1]

[1] I have not tried to reproduce the sonnet form, only to give something of its measured pace. (D.L.)

à François Billoux

Ni les fleurs, ni vos filles
Ne nous font un rempart

Contre vos tentacules
Où bougent des polices.

★

Lanternes d'or vous êtes
Au fond de longs couloirs
Dans vos bureaux de laine,

A ne rien éclairer,
A durer pour durer.

★

Vous pourrissez, vous pourrissez
Si lentement,

Et quand vous pourrissez
Ce n'est pas que sur vous.

★

Mais où est l'homme
Dans tout cela?

Pour qui
Ces paroles?

Neither flowers nor your daughters
make us a rampart

against your tentacles,
muscular with police.

★

You are gold lanterns
at the end of long corridors
in your woolen offices,

lighting nothing,
obstinately existing.

★

You rot, you rot
so slowly,

and when you rot
it is from within.

★

But where is man
in all this?

For whom
those words?

C'est pour des murs
Ou pour des hommes?

Pour des papiers
Ou pour des têtes?

Ils se réunissent
Comme un matériel.

Et ça vole et tue,
Par millions de corps.

★

Pour vous qu'il chantait,
L'absurde coucou.

Pour vous, au soleil,
Son cri répeté.

Pour vos coffres-forts
Et pour vos bureaux,

Le cri du coucou
Pareil à l'alcool.

★

Nous n'avons que faire
De vos plaisirs.

Nous n'avons que faire
De vos paroles.

Nous n'avons à faire
Que votre perte.

For walls
or men?

For paper
or for heads?

They join together
like something real.

And that something
steals and kills

in millions of bodies.

★

For you he sang,
the absurd cuckoo.

For you, in the sun,
his repeated cry.

For your strongboxes
and your offices,

the cuckoo's cry,
like strong liquor.

★

Your pleasures
mean nothing to us.

Your words
mean nothing to us.

To get rid of you
means something to us.

★

Voici les genêts
Et voici la mer.

Ecoutez un peu
Comment on vous dit:

Contre l'avenir
On ne force pas.

Ecoutez encore
Comment on vous dit:

Que trahison
Ne maintient pas.

★

De vous bureaux de laine
Vous convoquez le monde

Et vous serrez les mains
Sur le butin du jour.

Sur tous les points du globe
Vous pointez des épingles.

★

Vous n'avez pas de lieu,
Vous épinglez le globe.

Vos bureaux de velours
N'ont pas de paysage
Où s'attacher plutôt.

★

Here is the gorse
and the sea.

Listen a while,
something is saying to you:

Against the future
you can't do a thing.

Listen some more,
something is saying to you:

Treason
will not uphold you.

★

From your woolen offices
you convoke the world,

tightening your hands
around the day's loot.

All over the globe of the world
you stick pins.

★

You have no place of your own,
you stick pins in the globe.

Your velvet offices
have no landscape
in which they would belong.

25

Les quartiers sont en bas,
Très bas, très loin de vous.

★

Vous creusez du vide
Autour de chacun.

Vous posez des murs
Autour de chacun.

Vous aspirez tout
Et laissez du vide

Cerné par des murs,
Des idées de murs.

★

Bien entre vous,
sur tout le globe,

C'est l'un à l'autre
Et l'un dans l'autre,

Way down,
infinitely far from you,

are neighborhoods,
places where people live.[1]

★

You scoop out an emptiness
around each of you.

You put walls
around each of you.

You breathe-in everything
and leave voids

surrounded by walls,
by the idea of walls.

★

Among the lot of you,
all over the world,

the left hand washes the right,
you scratch one another's backs.

[1] The line, "places where people live" amplifies the word *neighborhoods*. Without such qualification, "neighborhoods" does not seem to me to carry the human associations of "quartier." If one is talking, saying for instance, "those two blocks of 95th Street have a real neighborhood feeling," then one is providing those associations by implication; but here "neighborhood" alone would not imply the contrast Guillevic is making between the offices of the Power Elite and the life of ordinary people experiencing some degree of human communion way below them. (D.L.)

Bol d'araignées
Mêlant leurs pattes,

Aussi leurs têtes,
Pour s'embrasser ou s'absorber.

★

Si c'est être vainqueur
Que réduire à merci

Ceux qui font à la terre
Donner ce qu'il vous faut,

Alors, vous êtes forts
Très souvent et vainqueurs.

★

Un corbeau bien vivant
Qu'on couperait en deux

Et les deux parties rouges
Qui se regarderaient,

C'est vous et nous.

★

Vous voyez tout d'en haut.
Vous dirigez d'en haut.

Vous regardez en bas,
Vous observez le bas.

A knot of spiders
intertwining their legs,

and their heads too,
to grasp each other,
to suck one another in.

★

If to be victor
is to crush at will

those who make earth yield
the things you need,

you are indeed, then,
often the victors.

★

A live crow
that's been cut in half,

whose two red halves
look at each other—

that's you and us.

★

You look down from a height.
You direct affairs from up there.

You look down, you observe
the lowly places.

C'est d'en bas,
En effet,

Que monteront les hommes
Avec de grand visages.

★

—Vous accrocher—
C'est votre lot.

Et nous il faut
Qu'on vous arrache.

★

Vous avouerez:
C'est plus qu'une brise
Qui remue entre vous
Les fils que vous tenez.

Orage et grand vent
Sur le capital.

And indeed,
it is from down there

that there will rise
the men with open faces.

★

You dig in—
it's your way.

And we're going to have to
dig you out.

★

You will admit it's more than a breeze
shaking in you the cord
you hold on to.

Storm and high wind
over the capital.

Les mains,
C'est les acides.

Les jambes,
C'est la station debout.

Le teint,
C'est cette espèce de nourriture

Et la toux,
C'est les vapeurs de l'usine
Et l'habitat.

Belle pourtant, belle
A donner courage.

C'est le regard
De ces yeux qu'elle a.

The hands,
that's the acid.

The legs,
that's the standing.

The skin-color,
that's the lousy food.

And the cough,
that's the factory fumes,
the dump she lives in.

Beautiful, though; a beauty
that gives one courage.

It's the look
in those eyes of hers.

à Maria Théresa Leon et à Rafael Alberti

Un silence, Espagne, un silence et rien
Que ce trou noir et froid dans un coin de mémoire.

Espagne, il y en a
Qui n'ont pas don pour écouter.

Il y en a qui ne croient pas
Et c'est les mêmes.

Ils ne croient qu'au malheur
Et ça les mène loin,

Jusqu'à des routes
Où tu n'es pas.

Il y en a qui ont été
Jusqu'à confondre, c'est leur crime,
Ton silence avec ton secret.

A silence, Spain, a silence and nothing
but this black, cold hole in a corner of memory.

Spain, there are people
with no gift for listening.

There are people without belief
and they are the same ones.

They believe only in sorrow,
and that leads them far away,

away to roads
where you are not.

There are some who have been
so far away they confound—and that's their crime—
your silence with your secret.

Meurent dans des collines
Que je ne connais guère

Des hommes de chez nous
Que je n'ai pas connus.

★

Meurent dans des collines
Que je ne connais guère

Des hommes d'Algérie
Que je ne connais pas.

★

Que je connais peut-être
A travers d'autres hommes
Que je connais un peu

Et je les cherche dans ceux-ci.

★

C'est à ceux qu'on rencontre,
A ceux qui ont visage encore,

Qu'on demande pardon
Pour ceux qui n'en n'ont plus.

Among the hills I hardly knew
there die

men from home
whom I did not know.

★

Among the hills I hardly knew
there die

men from Algeria
whom I did not know.

★

Whom I did know, perhaps,
through other men whom
I knew a little;

and I look for them
in these others.

★

It is of those one encounters,
those who still have faces,

that one asks forgiveness
for those who have lost theirs.

à Pierre Daix

Nous entrions parfois dans des cafés secrets
Sur le bord de la route.

Il pouvait y avoir une marche à descendre,
Il y avait toujours une table à choisir
Dans le silence ou le murmure des paroles.

L'ombre y était la plus ancienne des habitués,
Elle avait occupé toutes les places longuement.

Le soleil était là en accord avec elle,
Se posait sur un front, sur ta main, sur un verre
Et s'en allait bientôt comme un dieu qu'on oublie.

Pendant la halte qui semblait s'éterniser,
De l'expérience nous venait

Et nous sortions toujours de ces cafés secrets
Pas tout à fait les mêmes qu'en entrant.

Sometimes we used to enter
secret wayside cafés.

There might be a step down,
and always there was a table to choose
in the silence or the murmur of speech.

A shadow was the most ancient of the regulars;
a long, long time she had sat at every place.

The sun would be there, on good terms with her,
lying upon a forehead, on your hand, on a glass—
and soon he left, like a god one forgets.

During these halts that seemed to become eternal
experience came to us,

and we always left these secret cafés
subtly changed from what we had been before.

Comme si tu croyais
Que je ne te suis rien,

Si tu ne savais pas
Que j'ai fait avec toi
Ces fruits qui t'ont mûri,

Si tu ne savais pas
Que je vais avec toi
Dans le plus de possible,

Comme si tu voulais
Désavouer, cacher.

Nous ne sommes pourtant
Pas plus incestueux
Que d'autres qui se trouvent.

As if you believed
I were nothing to you,

as if you didn't know
it was I who made with you
those fruits that have ripened you,

as if you didn't know
that I go with you
into the more than possible,

as if you wanted
to disavow, to hide.

And yet we are
no more incestuous
than others who find each other.

Qu'est-ce que fait le chêne
Au long des chemins creux
Ou dans l'obscur du bois?

La cognée sera prête
Avant que tu sois prêt
Et faite avec ton bois.

L'hécatombe est dans l'air
A l'abri du silence.

What is the oak doing
along the empty lanes
and in the dark of the woods?

The axe will be ready
before you are ready and done
with your wood.

Sacrifice pends
under cover of silence.

Ce qui n'est pas dans la pierre,
Ce qui n'est pas dans le mur de pierre et de terre,
Même pas dans les arbres,
Ce qui tremble toujours un peu,

Alors, c'est dans nous.

Un Clou

Le clou
N'est qu'un peu rouillé.

Il n'a pas dû servir encore.
Il reposait
Comme on repose.

Il est de ceux qui font
Ce silence parti
A sa propre recherche.

That which is not in stone,
not in the wall of stones and earth,
not even in trees,
that which forever trembles a little,

must, then, be in us.

A Nail

The nail
is only the least bit rusted.

It has not had to serve yet.
It has been resting,
the way one rests.

It's one of the things that make
this silence gone
in search of itself.

Fait pour ma main,
Je te tiens bien.
Je me sens fort
De notre force.

Tu dors longtemps,
Tu sais le noir,
Tu as sa force.

Je te touche et te pèse,
Je te balance,
Je te chauffe au creux de ma main.

Je remonte avec toi
Dans le fer et le bois.

Tu me ramènes,
Tu veux
T'essayer,
Tu veux frapper.

You're made for my hand,
I get a firm grip on you,
and feel
strong in our strength.

You sleep a lot,
you know what black is,
its force is your force.

I touch you, weigh you, balance you,
warm you in the hollow of my hand.

I return with you
into iron and wood.

But you pull me back:
you want
to try yourself,
to strike.

Peut-être que le monde est mort
A l'instant même,

Que tout a basculé dans une autre lumière
Qui rassemble assez bien
A celle d'autrefois.

Il reste un simulacre
De murs et de rochers
Où tu vas sans l'histoire.

A moins qu'un homme vienne
Et sourie en passant.

Battement

Pas d'aile, pas d'oiseau, pas de vent, mais la nuit,
Rien que le battement d'une absence de bruit.

Perhaps this very moment
the world has died,

everything sunk under a different light
like enough to
the old light.

A simulacrum remains
of walls and rocks
where you move without history.

Unless a man appears
and smiles as he goes by.

Heartbeat

Not a wing, not a bird, no wind, but night,
only the pulsing of soundlessness.

Parfois les nuits sont si claires
Qu'elles sont comme un appel.

Il peut y avoir tellement d'étoiles
Que dans ce fouillis solennel

A peine si tu distingues
Çà et là quelques étoiles:
Celles qui sont condamnées.

Le Soleil

Le soleil jamais
Ailleurs qu'en lui-même
Ne verra la nuit,

Puisque ce noir qu'il jette
Caille en lumière
Autour de lui.

Turmoil of Stars

Sometimes the nights are so clear
they're like a call.

On such nights there are so many stars
that in that solemn turmoil

you can hardly distinguish
here and there single stars:
those that are condemned.

The Sun

The sun will never—
save within himself
—see the night,

for that blackness he spurts out
curdles to light
all around him.

L'éternité
ne fut jamais perdue.

Ce qui nous a manqué
Fut plutôt de savoir

La traduire en journées,
En ciels, en paysages,

En paroles pour d'autres,
En gestes vérifiables.

Mais la garder pour nous
N'était pas difficile

Et les moments étaient présents
Où nous paraissait clair
Que nous étions l'éternité.

Eternity
never was lost.

What we did not know

was how to translate it into days,
skies, landscapes,

into words for others,
authentic gestures.

But holding on to it for ourselves,
that was not difficult,

and there were moments
when it seemed clear to us
we ourselves were eternity.

Le repos du dimanche après-midi
Dans la campagne, avec le coq encore
A crier sa furie.

Il n'y a pas un autre monde
Pour le repos.

Il y a ce silence autour du coq,
La saison qui s'arrête
Avant d'autres violences.

Sauvage est le passage
Intouchable des heures,
Sauvage le besoin de parler aux étangs,
De n'être pas en reste avec le cri du coq.

Mais le repos parfois
Vient nous toucher la face.

A Sunday afternoon rest
in the country, the cock
still crowing his fury.

There is no other world
in which to rest.

There is this silence that surrounds the cock,
the season pausing
before further violence.

Savage the untouchable
passing of the hours,
savage the need to speak to the ponds,
to match the cry of the cock.

But repose sometimes
comes to touch our faces.

Dans la lumière du plein jour
Il y a des grottes.

Dans le plein soleil
Il y a des grottes.

Il n'est pas toujours
Mauvais de s'y rendre,

De s'y résumer,
De venir ensuite,

Chargé d'autre chose,
Consacrer le jour.

In the full light of day
there are caves.

In full sunlight,
caverns.

It's not always
a bad thing to enter them,

to think oneself over in there,
and emerge then

charged with something else,
to hallow the day.

Pour elles c'est la faim,
L'espace de la faim

Et le temps de crier
L'espace avec leur faim,

Le temps de promener
L'espace dans leur faim,

D'accompagner la mer,
De maudire la mer

Qui ne sait pas borner
L'espace ni la faim.

Life for them is hunger,
vast spaces of hunger,

and time to cry out space
through their hunger,

time to lead
space into their hunger,

to drift with the sea,
to curse the sea

that will not set bounds
to space and hunger.

Il n'y a pas que toi,
Coquelicot.

Ce besoin qui te fait
Eclater dans le rouge,
Etaler des pétales,

Ce besoin de clamer
Par ta forme et le rouge
Que la vie est ici
A prendre sur le vif,

Ce besoin de chanter
Que tu y réussis,

Prête-le donc à d'autres,
Et du temps pour le vivre.

There is nothing but you,
field-poppy.

This need you have
to flare forth in scarlet,
to display your petals,

this need to assert,
by your openness,[1] by redness,
that life is here to be taken
alive and kicking,

this need to sing out
that you're a success—

give us a share of it,
and time to live it.

[1] Literally, "by your form." But what characterizes the form of a poppy once its bud has unfurled is its wide-openness, the bold abandon of the loosely attached, delicate silky petals, so vulnerable to wind and rain. (D.L.)

Comme si quelque chose
Marchait auprès de toi,
T'accompagnait.

Là, de l'autre côté
D'une espèce de vitre,
Il ne te quitte pas.

Il est là qui regarde
Et l'on dirait que c'est
Son devoir, sa passion.

Il est pour que tu ailles.
Il t'allège le corps
Ainsi qu'un appel d'air.

Sans lui d'ailleurs,
Tu n'irais pas.

Tu croulerais
Si du futur

Ne te visait.

As if something
walked beside you,
kept you company.

There, on the other side
of some kind of glass;
it doesn't leave you.

That which watches
keeps pace—it seems
its duty, its passion.

That you may move,
it lightens your body for you
as if the air summoned you.

And indeed, without it
you would not budge.

You would founder[1]
if the future did not

keep you in sight.

[1] Literally "crumble" or "crumple." (D.L.)

à Aurora Cornu

A tous les horizons,
Mère, tu m'attendais
Pour demander des comptes.

Et je ne voulais pas,
J'avais à faire.

D'autres m'appellent,
Rêvent de joie.

La terre est lourde, me prendra.
En attendant elle est en moi.

Et je la porte,
Je la fais entrer dans nos fêtes.

Celle que j'aime
Te le dira.

Vaste est le jour.

Je le dépasse
A travers elle.

At every horizon,
mother, you used to wait for me
to demand a reckoning.

And I would not give it,
I had things to do.

Others call me,
dream of joy.

The earth is heavy, it will take me.
Meanwhile it is in me.

And I carry it,
I give it entry to our festivals.

She whom I love
will tell you so.

Vast is the day.

Through her
I overtake it.

à Georges Somlyo

Prenez un toit de vieilles tuiles
Un peu après midi.

Placez tout à côté
Un tilleul déjà grand
Remué par le vent,

Mettez au-dessus d'eux
Un ciel de bleu, lavé
Par des nuages blancs.

Laissez-les faire.
Regardez-les.

Take a roof of old tiles
a short while after midday.

Place nearby
a fullgrown linden
stirred by the wind.

Above them put
a blue sky washed
by white clouds.

Let them be.[1]
Watch them.

---

[1] I was tempted to translate the penultimate line as, "Let them simmer," or even "Let them work"—thinking of, for instance, the setting aside of bread-dough to rise, and of certain other culinary procedures.
(D.L.)

à Paul Chaulot

Enquête No. 1

Est-ce que la lumière
Vous a fait mal?

Est-ce que la lumière
Parfois vous emporte?

Est-ce que c'est toujours
La même lumière?

Enquête No. 2

Avez-vous une fleur
Que vous préférez?

La fleur le sait-elle?

D'après vous, comment
L'aura-t-elle appris?

Enquête No. 3

La force de qui,
La force de quoi,
Rêvez-vous d'avoir?

Et c'est pour quoi faire?

1

Has the light
done you any injury?

Does the light
ever take you away?

Is it always
the same light?

2

Have you
a flower you prefer?

Does the flower know this?

According to you,
how would the flower
have learned of your preference?

3

The strength of whom,
the strength of what,
do you dream of having?

And for what purpose?

Est-ce que le futur
Est pour vous présent?

Est-il un plafond
Auquel vous cognez?

Est-il autre chose?
Est-il familier?

S'il prend trop de place
Où vous mettez-vous?

Enquête No. 5

Avez-vous été
L'herbe que l'on foule?

Saviez-vous pourquoi
L'on passait par là?

Enquête No. 6

Quand vous avez choisi
D'être telle couleur,

Que faites-vous des autres?

4

Is the future
present for you?

Is it a ceiling
on which you knock?

Is it something else?
Is it familiar?

If it takes too much space,
where do you put yourself?

5

Have you been
the grass one treads on?

Did you know why
one stepped just there?

6

When you have chosen to be
one certain color,

what do you do with the rest?

Enquête No. 7

Si vous étiez le géranium
En pot sur la fenêtre,

Voudriez-vous avoir
Plus de fleurs, plus de feuilles?

Enquête No. 8

Quand vous êtes la nuit
Qui saisit les campagnes,

Que vous promettez-vous
Qui vous étonnerait?

Enquête No. 9

Quand vous voyez le ciel
Regarder nos journées,

N'avez-vous pas pensé
Qu'il aurait mieux à faire?

7

If you were the geranium
in a pot at the window,

would you have
more flowers, more leaves?

8

When you are the night
that grips the countryside,

what do you promise yourself
that would astonish you?

9

When you see the sky
watching our days,

have you not thought it should have
something better to do?

Est-ce que le soleil
Vous quitte sans regret?

S'en est-il expliqué?

Enquéte No. 11

S'il y avait un Dieu
Et qu'il n'existerait
Que la nuit, pas le jour,

Voudriez-vous dormir
Dans le monde avec Dieu?
Dans le monde sans Dieu?

Même question pour le réveil.

10

Does the sun
depart from you without regret?

Has the sun
explained this?

11

If there were a God
and he existed
only at night, not by day,

would you sleep
in the world with God?
in the world without God?

Same question for waking.

1

Ils ne le sauront pas les rocs,
Qu'on parle d'eux.

Et toujours ils n'auront pour tenir
Que grandeur.

Et que l'oubli de la marée,
Des soleils rouges.

2

Ils n'ont pas le besoin du rire
Ou de l'ivresse.

Ils ne font pas brûler
Du soufre dans le noir.

Car jamais
Ils n'ont craint la mort.

De la peur
Ils ont fait un hôte.

Et leur folie
Est clairvoyante.

1

The rocks won't know
one speaks about them.

And always to sustain them, they'll have
only grandeur.

And the oblivion of the marshes,
the red suns.

2

They have no need of laughter,
no need to get drunk.

They don't burn sulphur
in the darkness

for they have never known
the fear of death.

They have entertained
fear as a guest.

Their madness
is clairvoyant.

3

Et puis la joie

De savoir la menace
Et de durer.

Pendant que sur les bords,
De la pierre les quitte

Que la vague et le vent grattaient
Pendant leur sieste.

4

Ils n'ont pas à porter leur face
Comme un supplice.

Ils n'ont pas à porter de face
Où tout se lit.

5

La danse est en eux,
La flamme est en eux,
Quand bon leur semble.

Ce n'est pas un spectacle devant eux,
C'est en eux.

C'est la dance de leur intime
Et lucide folie.

3

And then the joy

of knowing the menace
and enduring.

While at their edges
bits of stone flake off

which wind and wave had scraped at
while they were dozing.

4

They don't have to bear their faces
like supplications.

They don't have to go about
With faces you can read like books.

5

The dance is within them,
the flame is within them,
when it seems good to them.

Not as a spectacle before them,
but in them.

The dance of their intimate
and lucid madness.

C'est la flamme en eux
Du noyau de braise.

6

Ils n'ont pas voulu être le temple
Où se complaire.

Mais la menace est toujours là
Dans le dehors.

Et la joie
Leur vient d'eux seuls,

Que la mer soit grise
Ou pourrie de bleue.

7

Ils sentent le dehors,
Ils savent le dehors.

Peut-être parfois l'auront-ils béni
De les limiter:

La toute puissance
N'est pas leur faible.

8

Parfois dans leur nuit
C'est un grondement
Qui longtemps résonne.

The flame in them
of the live coal's core.

6

They did not want to be the temple
in which to delight.

But the menace is there always
in what's outside them.

And joy
comes to them out of themselves alone,

whether the sea is gray or
tainted with blue.

7

They feel the external,
they know the external.

Perhaps sometimes they would have counted it blessèd
to limit their knowledge:

omnipotence
is not their weakness.

8

Sometimes by night
sounds and resounds
a long muttering.

Et leur grain se noie
Dans un vaste effroi:

Ils ne savaient plus
Qu'ils avaient une voix.

9

Il arrive qu'un bloc
Se détache et tombe,

Tombe à perdre haleine
Dans la mer liquide.

Ils n'étaient donc bien
Que des blocs de pierre,

Un lieu de la danse
Que la danse épuise.

10

Mais le pire est toujours
D'être en dehors de soi
Quand la folie
N'est plus lucide.

D'être le souvenir d'un roc et l'étendue
Vers le dehors et vers le vague.

And their particles
are flooded with terror:

they had not still known
they had a voice.

9

It happens that a block of stone
detaches itself and falls,

falls so that one misses a breath,
into the wet sea.

Well, they were only
blocks of stone,

a dancing-place
worn out by the dance.

10

But the worst is always
to be beside onself
when madness
is no longer lucid.

To be the memory of a rock, of being
promontory, out and towards the wave.

Apporte au crépuscule
Quelques herbes d'ici.
Quand le soleil bascule
Dis-lui, dis-lui merci.

Tends-lui la renoncule
Et le brin de persil.
Les choses minuscules
Il les connaît aussi.

To the twilight, bring
some herbs that grow here.
As the sun goes down, sing
to him, give thanks.

Offer the sun
a sprig of parsley,
a buttercup. He too is one
who has known these small things.

Je vois, mes composants:
Vous en avez assez.

Il y a bien longtemps
Que vous êtes mon corps.

Vous avez trop connu
Le tremblement, la frénésie.

Vous avez grand besoin
D'avoir un autre état:

Quelque part molécules
Bâillant, batifolant

Dans l'air, le minéral,
Dans n'importe quelle eau.

Ça ne vous fait trop rien,
Vous, un assassinat.

My Components

I see, my components:
you've had enough.

It's been a long time now
you've been my body.

You know too much
about trembling, about frenzy.

You've a great need
for different conditions:

somewhere molecules
are yawning, fooling around

in air, in minerals,
in water—no matter where.

You don't give a damn
about murder, do you?

Ce n'est pas moi
Qui fermerai,

Pas moi qui crierai
Pour la fermeture.

C'est qu'on me fermera.

★

La lavande
Est passée dans l'air,

Voulait rester.

★

Ici
L'air est coupant

Comme ce qui sera
Pour la fin de tes jours.

★

Ciel bleu, ciel grand,
Te regardant,

Je suis bien
Lorsque je suis toi,

De mon vivant.

Of My Death

It is not I
who will close,

not I who will demand
that I be closed.

Something will close me.

★

Lavender
passed by in the breeze,

wanted to stay.

★

Here
the air is sharp-edged

like the air will be
at the end of your days.

★

Blue sky, great sky,
watching you,

I am content—
so long as I am you—
with my span of life.

★

Je m'étais endormi
Dans les destins de l'herbe.

Je n'en avais plus.

★

C'est aujourd'hui, j'avais seize ans,
Que tu es mince et blanche sur ton lit,
Etendue au milieu des couronnes de perles.

C'est aujourd'hui que j'ai,
Pour vivre, ton amour.

★

Pâlotte fleur,
Ce qu'il en reste.

Le vent, la pluie,
Si peu d'égards.

★

Le pigeon qui venait
Mourir auprès de toi,

Qui mourait dans l'espace
Où tu devras mourir.

★

I fell asleep
among the destinies of the grass.

Had no more
destiny of my own.

★

It's today that I was sixteen,
and you white and slender on your bed,
stretched among crowns of pearl.

It's today I have,
for life, your love.

★

A pallid flower
is what's left.

The wind, the rain,
a carelessness.

★

The pigeon who came
to die near to you,

who died in the space where
you must die.

★

Je t'écoute, prunier.

Dis-moi ce que tu sais
Du terme qui déjà
Vient se figer en toi.

★

Si cela pouvait être
Aussi satisfaisant,
Aussi doux que laisser
Le sommeil me contraindre,

Cependant que j'aurais
Conscience encore un peu
D'aider l'envahisseur

Vers l'îlot qui sera
Le dernier à livrer.

★

Il faudrait accepter

Pas la mort,
Mais la mienne.

★

L'autre temps,
Celui-là qui n'est pas au présent,

Tournait autour de moi
Sa gueule qui a faim.

★

I'm listening, plum tree.

Tell me what you know
of the term that has already
been set within you.

★

If it could be
as satisfying, as sweet
as to let sleep constrain me,

and yet if I could stay
conscious a while longer
to help the invader

towards that small islet which will be
the last to surrender.

★

One must accept

not *death*
but *my death.*

★

That other time,
that which is not at present,

turned towards me
its hungry jaws.

★

Du moins je n'aurai pas
A me connaître alors,

Pas à me voir cadavre.

★

J'ai possédé parfois
Le volume et la courbe,

La vôtre avec la mienne,

Et j'ai tout enfermé
Dans la sphère qui dure,

Qui pourrait durer plus
Si je n'y mettais fin
Pour encore essayer.

★

Si elle avait voulu

Tout autant de moi
Que je voulais d'elle,
Ma terre,

Il n'y aurait pas eu
De terme à notre amour.

★

At least I won't have to
know myself then,

won't have to see my own corpse.

★

I have possessed at times
volume and curve,

yours as well as mine,

and I've enclosed them all
in a durable sphere

which could last still longer
if I didn't stop it
to try again.

★

If she had wanted

as much from me
as I from her,
my earth,

there would have been no
limit to our love.

Au bord le plus souvent
De quelque chose de géant
Qui m'en voudrait.

Parfois après l'à-pic
Et parfois de plain-pied,

Quelque chose de clos
De hérissé, de lourd,
Qui serait là.

Un poème peut-être
Ou la fin de mes jours.

★

Parce qu'il y a terme
A ces jours devant toi,

Que d'aller vers ce terme
Fait par-dessous tes jours
Un creux qui les éclaire,

Tu as le goût
De ces rapports qui sont de joie
Avec les murs et le rosier.

★

Le voyage était là, partout,
Le voyage était de toujours.

La profondeur environnait,
Parfois s'ouvrait.

★

At the edge most often
of something giant
that is at odds with me.

Sometimes after the steep,
sometimes the level,

something shut in,
bristled, heavy,
which will be there.

A poem perhaps
or the end of my days.

★

Because there is a term
to the days ahead of you

and moving towards that term
scoops out a hollow under the days,
from which they are illumined,

you have a taste for
those rapports with the walls
and with the roses, which is joy.

★

Everywhere, the voyage.
Always, the voyage.

Depth surrounding,
sometimes opening.

Hasardeuses
Etaient les étapes,

Le but gardé
Comme un secret.

★

M'endormant chaque soir
En me voyant gratter
Ce côté-ci de la surface.

★

Toute une vie
Avec un terme

Comme un loyer,
Comme un trimestre,

Dont meurt un pin,
Dont meurt un homme.

Tout une vie
Pour faire en sorte

Qu'il ne soit pas,
Qu'il soit passé.

★

Qu'elle soit longue, au moins,
Cette vie qu'il faut vivre.

Car difficile
Est la leçon.

Each lap of the journey
dangerous,

the destination
kept secret.

★

Falling asleep each evening
seeing myself scraping
this side of the surface.

★

A whole life
with a set term

like the rent,
like a trimester;

from which a pine is dying,
from which a man is dying.

A whole life
to ensure

that it shan't be,
that it shall be over.

★

May it be long, at least,
this life one has to live.

For difficult
is the lesson.

★

Si quelque chose pour la fin
Veut se garder,
Comment savoir?

Et s'il n'y avait pas
De grand dernier moment?

Si la fin
N'avait pas de bord?

Si tout s'abandonnait
Avant d'arriver là
Ou si c'était soudain?

★

Tu ne t'es pas pour rien
Ecartelé au long des jours
Sur toutes les courbes.

Tu en as ramené
Ce gibier tremblotant
Que tu tiens pour donner.

★

Quand je ne serai plus,

Les rochers porteront
Plus lourd qu'ils n'ont porté,

Le jour tâtonnera
Plus inquiet vers la mer.

★

If something wants to keep itself
for the end,
how would one know it?

And if there were
no great final moment?

If the end
has no edge of beginning?

If all were to surrender
before arriving there,
or it were sudden?

★

Not for nothing have you swerved
into every turn of your road.

You have brought back
this shuddering wild bird
you hold out
            to give away.

★

When I am gone

the rocks will bear themselves
more heavily than what they once bore,

the day stumble
more troubled towards the sea.

Peut-être que l'abeille
Volera tout pareil,

Mais les fleurs recevront
En amie la rosée.

La boue des chemins creux
N'attendra plus autant,

La carrière craindra
Un peu plus de midi.

Il manquera ce lien
Entre tous ceux qui pèsent.

Je ne remplirai plus
Les gouffres qui voudront
Se remplir avec vous.

Vous m'accuserez tous
De ne plus être là.

★

Si ce sera monter
Vers le point terminal,
Si ce sera descendre,

La question
Restera posée.

Et c'est peut-être encore
Accorder trop de sens

Perhaps the bee's flight
won't change

but the flowers will welcome
dewfall.

The mud of deep lanes
will dry up sooner,

the quarries will fear noon
just a bit more.

That line will be missing
that links all those who have weight.

I shall no longer fill
those gulfs that desire
to fill themselves with you.

All of you will accuse me
of not being here any more.

★

Whether to reach the point
of ending one goes
up or down

is an open question.

And maybe
to assume any direction

A ce qui peut
N'en pas avoir,

Ennoblir
De l'horreur.

★

Et pourtant comme si
Ce que je dis ici,
Ce que je cherche à dire

N'avait rien de commun
Avec ce qui sera
Le terme de mes jours,

La fin définitive
D'une vie qui vivait,

Cette inimaginable fin
D'une épopée
Dans le plus rien.

Car tout ce que je touche
Tourne autour
Sans toucher.

where there may be none

is to accord nobility
to horror.

★

And yet it's as if
what I am saying here,
what I'm seeking to say,

had nothing in common with
what the end of my days
will be,

the definitive end
of a life that lived.

That unimaginable end
of an epic
in the *nothing more*.

For all I touch
turns about
without touching.

Mésange Morte

Parle-t-on de toi
Quelque part encore
Parmi les tiens?

Dit-on le nom?

Cerisier

Te voici devenu,
Comme ce fut rêvé,

Rien que cette blancheur
Effrayant l'horizon,

Rien que la fiancée
Préparée pour les noces.

Qui te prendra?
Qui doit venir?

Dead Titmouse

Is there still talk of thee,
somewhere,
among thy kinsfolk?

Is thy name
still spoken?

Cherry Tree

As it was dreamed you would,
you have become

no other than that whiteness
startling the horizon,

no other than the bride
prepared for the wedding.

Who is it
will come to take you?

On aurait pu bénir le jardin, la journée
Où les choses vont lentement
Dans la lumière du mois d'août.

Tombent les reines-claudes, les voici
Cernées par le bourdonnement
Qui dit l'achèvement peut-être.

Et ce serait dans le silence
Qui ne ressemble pas à d'autres,
Dans l'éblouissement de l'amitié finale.

Blessèd the garden, the day
where things go slow
in the light of August.

The sweet plums fall, they lie
encircled by a buzzing
that speaks perhaps
of completion.

And that shall come to pass
in silence unlike all other silence,
dizziness of a final friendship.

Je ne parle pas pour moi,
Je ne parle pas en mon nom,
Ce n'est pas de moi qu'il s'agit.

Je ne suis rien
Qu'un peu de vie, beaucoup d'orgueil.

Je parle pour tout ce qui est,
Au nom de tout ce qui a forme et pas de forme.
Il s'agit de tout ce qui pèse,
De tout ce qui n'a pas de poids.

Je sais que tout a volonté, autour de moi,
D'aller plus loin, de vivre plus,
De mieux mourir aussi longtemps
Qu'il faut mourir.

Ne croyez pas entendre en vous
Les mots, la voix de Guillevic.

C'est la voix du présent allant vers l'avenir
Qui vient de lui sous votre peau.

I don't speak for myself,
I don't speak in my name,
it's not a question of me.

I'm nothing but
a little life, a lot of pride.

I speak for all that is,
in the name of all that has form and no form.
It's a question of all that weighs
and all that's weightless.

I know that everything that surrounds me
longs to go further, to live more intensely,
to die more fully, if dying
is what must be done.

Don't think you hear inside you
the words and the voice of Guillevic.

It's the voice of the present moving towards the future,
the voice of the present sounding from under your skin.

1

La pierre qui n'a pas
Besoin de résonner,

La fleur de géranium
Qui veille en permanence,

La bûche qui s'étonne
De devenir la flamme,

Le vent qui se souvient
N'avoir été que ciel,

La plaine effarouchée
D'aboutir dans un cri.

4

La moisson se devine
Au silence des fermes,

Au regard de la femme
Qui traverse la cour.

5

De toutes les larves
Révélées au jour en levant les pierres,
Les morceaux de bois,

from **Elegy of the Forest of Sainte-Croix**

1

The stone that has no need
to make any sound,

the geranium flower
keeping unbroken vigil,

the log astonished
at becoming flame,

the wind remembering
having been only sky,

the plain startled to find itself
ending as utterance.

4

Harvest-time is revealed
in the silence around the farmhouse,

the look of the woman
crossing the farmyard.

5

Among all the grubs
revealed to daylight as you dislodge
a stone, a fallen branch,

Aucune qui veuille
Que ça dure encore
Le vivre à demi.

6

Si, moi qui parle terre,
Qui parle espace et noir,

Je m'en venais la nuit
Vous chercher dans vos lits?

Je viens peut-être.

8

Ne dis pas que le jour est pareil à la nuit.
Ne dis pas que la nuit est étrangère au jour.

Un voile tout pareil est tissé sur les choses
Et parfois se déchire

Dans la clarté du jour
Et le noir de la nuit.

10

Encore le coucou
Clame à travers les bois.

Encore le coucou
Se nomme dans le bois.

not one who would wish
that half-life
to continue.

6

I who talk earth,
who talk space and blackness,

what if I came at night
seeking you in your beds?

Perhaps I will come.

8

Don't say that day is the same as night.
Don't say that night is alien to day.

A single veil is woven across all things
and tears sometimes

in day's brightness
or night's black.

10

Again the cuckoo
clamors through the woods.

Again the cuckoo
calls his own name in the woods.

Ce n'est peut-être pas,
Pour lui-même et pour nous,

Selon que la lumière
Ouvre ou ferme les noces,

Toujours la même chose
Qu'il nomme dans le bois,

Mais c'est toujours l'humus
Demandant la parole.

13

Le coucou c'est aussi,
Plus lointain, plus profond,

Quelque chose qui veut
Entrouvrir, agrandir

Un espace où régner.

17

Qui, pendant qu'il criait
Pour s'arracher la nuit,
A tenu dans sa main
Le cou gonflé du coq?

116

Perhaps, neither for us nor for himself
—according to whether the light

opens or closes
the bridal feast—

is it always the same thing
he names in the woods,

but it's always the black earth
asking to speak.

13

The cuckoo also,
further away, deeper,

is a thing that wants
to open up, to extend

a space to rule in.

17

Who, while the cock was crowing
to root out night,
has put his hand around its
distended throat?

18

Et certes ce fut pire.

Ce n'était pas écrit
A ce niveau d'horreur.

Et le sous-sol du mal
Etait de l'inédit.

Mais la trouée,
Mais l'ouverture:

Ce chant d'un fou
Pour la raison.

19

Quel tremblement ce fut,
Le groseillier.

C'était en mai.
Le soleil était haut déjà,
Les insectes étaient ailleurs

Et lui tremblait.

20

Et celui qui tremblait
Ne tremblait pas pour lui.

Et celui qui tremblait
Tremblait pour bien plus grand.

18

Indeed it has been worse.

Unwritten,
that level of horror.

Unpublished,
that subsoil of evil.

But the aperture,
but the opening:

that hymn of a madman
to Reason.

19

What a trembling it made,
the gooseberry bush.

It was May.
The sun was already high,
the insects were somewhere else.

And he trembled.

20

And he who trembled
did not tremble for himself.

And he who trembled
trembled for something much greater.

Il n'était rien, en somme,
Que ce qu'en lui d'autres deviennent.

21

Le voile sur les choses,
Un tremblement toujours.

N'être que tremblement
De la plaine au matin.

22

Aussi la fleur sans nom
Egarée dans la terre
Qu'on n'a pas labourée

Dit que parler c'est pour donner
Ce que l'on croit ne pas avoir.

23

Ma folie
Est de ce monde.

24

Et voilà: j'étais pierre,
Je n'étais pas changé.

Simply, in fact, for what
others became in him.

21

The veil over all things,
an unceasing quivering.

To be no more
than a quivering of the flat distance,
mornings.

22

The nameless flower
astray in the patch of
waste ground

says that speech is for giving what one
doesn't believe one has.

23

My mad passion
is of this world.

24

And behold: I was stone,
and unchanged.

Pourtant je n'avais pas
A me traîner partout.

J'étais toujours au centre
Il y avait un chant

Que j'entendais toujours,
Quand j'en avais envie.

25

Pas de saisons.
J'ai la durée.

Dans ma maison,
Vivons la pierre.

Ça chante encore.
Je règne encore.

Et si ce n'est pas en moi-même,
Je règne ailleurs

Où je me donne rendez-vous
Et me retrouve.

26

Vienne le vent
Porteur de graines,
De cris d'oiseaux!

Still, I didn't have to
drag myself about any more.

I was always
at the very center.

There was a song
I heard always,

whenever I wanted to.

25

No seasons.
I last.

In my house
we live stone.

That sings on.
I reign still.

And if not within myself,
I reign elsewhere,

making appointments there
to meet myself,
and keeping them.

26

The wind comes,
bringer of seeds,
of bird-cries!

Entre le vent
Là ou tu viens
Pour t'enfermer!

27

La plaine, les vallons plus loin,
Les bois, les fleurs des champs,

Les chemins, les villages,
Les blés, les betteraves,

Le chant du merle et du coucou,
L'air chaud, les herbes, les tracteurs,

Les ramiers sur un bois,
Les perdrix, la luzerne,

L'allée des arbres sur la route,
La charrette immobile,

L'horizon, tout cela
Comme au creux de la main.

28

Le ronron d'un tracteur
Accompagne en silence
Le silence des champs.

Tout le travail se fait
Sous terre et sur le sol,

The wind enters
into that place where you think to
shut yourself in!

27

The plain, the little valleys beyond,
the woods, the wildflowers,

the roads, the villages,
the wheat, the beetfields,

the blackbird's song and the cuckoo's,
the warm air, the grass, the tractors,

the woodpigeons in the woods,
the pheasants, the clover,

the row of trees by the road,
the stillness of a cart,

the horizon, all this
as if in the palm of the hand.

28

Purr of a tractor
accompanying in silence
the field's silence.

All the work done
under the earth and on it,

Par l'herbe, les racines,
Par les graines, par l'eau,
Par la charrue, la herse,

Pour donner aux journées
Leur contenu de vie.

29

Quand les derniers coquelicots
Quittent la fête,

Reste la nôtre.

30

Le lièvre était toujours
A l'orée du bois.

La plaine toujours
Disait la rosée.

Le vent découvrait
La frayeur du lièvre.

Le chemin toujours
Allait vers le bois.

C'était toujours l'heure.

by grass, by roots,
by grains of wheat, by water,
by plow and hearse,

gives to the days
their content of life.

29

When the last poppies
leave the festival,

ours still lingers.

30

The hare was always
at the verge of the woods.

The plain always
spoke of dew.

The wind discovered
the hare's terror.

The road always
led to the woods.

The hour
had always come.

Parce que nous chantions
En demeurant à table,
En allant par les champs,

Parce que nous chantions
Parfois rien qu'en silence,
Rien que par le regard,

Nous gardions pour l'année
Ce qu'il faut de raison.

Et je ne serai plus
L'aiguillon de ces jours et le frein de ces nuits.

Je ne tremblerai plus
Quand le ciel blanchira.

Je ne porterai plus les premières lueurs,
Le corps de l'alouette, la frayeur du corbeau.

Je n'aurai plus à saluer
Les fleurs des champs, les innomées, les innombrables.

Et la terre sera,
Continuera la terre.

Demande-lui
Comment le croire.

Because we sang
at table and while we
walked through the fields,

because we sang
sometimes even in silence,
simply by looking,

we kept for the rest of the year
what sanity we needed.

And I shall no longer be
the goad of the days, the reiner-in of the nights.

I'll not tremble
any longer when the sky pales.

I'll bring the first gleams
of light no more, lark's body, crow's fear.

No more greeting
the wildflowers, the nameless, the innumerable.

And earth will be there,
earth will go on being there.

Ask it
how this can be.

34

Savoir nous fait porter
Tout le poids de nos gestes.

Dans l'espace, alors,
Nous faisons du plein.

Sur fond de ciel nous sommes
La marche des vivants.

35

Ah! soleil, ainsi tourne
Et tourne, mais quoi donc

De tout ce que tu livres
Au tremblement du jour.

38

Et celui qui tremblait
Attendait qu'on le croie.

40

Des chemins traversent les champs,
Des chemins traversent les bois.

Certains vont profond dans un bois
Et se perdent dans les taillis,

34

To know makes us carry
the full weight of our deeds.

Then we
fill our space.

Against the sky,
alive, moving.

35

Ah, sun, roll on, then,
but who knows

what shall become of
all you deliver into trembling day.

38

And he who trembled
was waiting to be believed.

40

Roads cross the fields,
roads cross the woods.

A few go into the depths of the forest
and lose themselves in the underbrush

Comme quelqu'un qui n'aurait pu
Sortir vivant d'être allé seul

Où l'on ne voulait pas de lui.

42

Pas recueilli
De résine du firmament.
Pas bu de lait d'étoiles.

Pas d'ascension.

44

Rassemble-toi.

Regarde-toi dans ta parole
Pour te tenir.

45

Est-ce que c'était toi le but,
O groseillier?

Es-tu la bouche?
Le résumé?

Arrive et donne.

like someone who could not survive having gone
alone into a place where no one wanted him.

42

Rosin of the firmament
not gathered.
Milk of the stars
not tasted.

No ascension.

44

Gather yourself together.

Look at yourself in your words,
and grasp yourself.

45

Were you the goal,
O gooseberry bush?

Are you the mouth?
the sum of all?

Arrive and give.

J'ai logé dans le merle.
Je crois savoir comment
Le merle se réveille et comment il veut dire
La lumière, du noir encore, quelques couleurs,
Leurs jeux lourds à travers
Ce rouge qu'il se voit.

J'ai fait leur verticale
Avec les blés.

Avec l'étang j'ai tâtonné
Vers le sommeil toujours tout proche.

J'ai vécu dans la fleur.
J'y ai vu le soleil
Venir s'occuper d'elle
Et l'inciter longtemps
A tenter ses frontières.

J'ai vécu dans des fruits
Qui rêvaient de durer.

J'ai vécu dans des yeux
Qui pensaient à sourire.

I have dwelt in the blackbird.
I believe I know
how the blackbird wakes, how he wants
to say the light, still part of
darkness, a few colors,
their heavy play across
that red he encounters within him.

Within the wheatstalks
I have sustained verticality.

With the pond I have wavered
towards sleep that is always nearby.

I have lived in a flower.
There I have seen the sun
approach to study the flower
and spend much time
inciting it to dare its own limits.

I have lived in fruit
that dreamed of enduring.

I have lived
in eyes that thought of smiling.

à Simone

Quand chacun de tes jours
Te sera sacré,

Quand chacune de tes heures
Te sera sacrée,

Quand chacun de tes instants
Te sera sacré,

Quand la terre et toi,
L'espace avec toi
Porterez le sacre
Au long de vos jours,

Alors tu seras
Dans le champ de gloire.

When each day
is sacred

when each hour
is sacred

when each instant
is sacred

earth and you
space and you
bearing the sacred
through time

you'll reach
the fields of light.[1]

[1] See Introduction, page xiv.

Requiem (Tschann, 1938)

Terraqué (Gallimard, 1942)

Exécutoire (Gallimard, 1947)

Gagner (Gallimard, 1949)

Les Chansons d'Antonin Blond (Seghers, 1949)

Envie de vivre (Seghers, 1951)

Terre à bonheur (Seghers, 1952)

31 Sonnets (Gallimard, 1954)

L'Age mûr (Cercle d'Art, 1955)

Carnac (Gallimard, 1961)

Sphère (Gallimard, 1963)

Avec (Gallimard, 1966)

Euclidiennes (Gallimard, 1967)

A selection of Guillevic's poems, with introduction by Jean Tortel, is also available in the "Poètes d'aujourdhui" series (Seghers, 1962).

Index of French titles and first lines

The small capitals following page numbers identify original editions, as follows: A–*Terraqué;* B–*Exécutoire;* C–*Gagner;* D–*31 Sonnets;* E–*Sphère;* F–*Avec.*

139

Index of English titles and first lines

141

New Directions Paperbooks

Y. Mishima, *Death in Midsummer*. NDP215.
  Confessions of a Mask. NDP253.
Eugenio Montale, *Selected Poems*.† NDP193.
Vladimir Nabokov, *Nikolai Gogol*. NDP78.
New Directions 17. (Anthology) NDP103.
New Directions 18. (Anthology) NDP163.
New Directions 19. (Anthology) NDP214.
New Directions 20. (Anthology) NDP248.
New Directions 21. (Anthology) NDP277.
Charles Olson, *Selected Writings*. NDP231.
George Oppen, *The Materials*. NDP122.
  Of Being Numerous. NDP245.
  This In Which. NDP201.
Wilfred Owen, *Collected Poems*. NDP210.
Nicanor Parra,
  Poems and Antipoems.† NDP242.
Boris Pasternak, *Safe Conduct*. NDP77.
Kenneth Patchen, *Because It Is*. NDP83.
  But Even So. NDP265.
  Collected Poems. NDP284.
  Doubleheader. NDP211.
  Hallelujah Anyway. NDP219.
  The Journal of Albion Moonlight. NDP99.
  Memoirs of a Shy Pornographer. NDP205.
  Selected Poems. NDP160.
  Sleepers Awake. NDP286.
Plays for a New Theater. (Anth.) NDP216.
Ezra Pound, *ABC of Reading*. NDP89.
  Classic Noh Theatre of Japan. NDP79.
  The Confucian Odes. NDP81.
  Confucius. NDP285.
  Confucius to Cummings. (Anth) NDP126.
  Guide to Kulchur. NDP257.
  Literary Essays. NDP250.
  Love Poems of Ancient Egypt. Gift Edition. NDP178.
  Selected Poems. NDP66.
  The Spirit of Romance. NDP266.
  Translations.† (Enlarged Edition) NDP145.
Philip Rahv, *Image and Idea*. NDP67.
Carl Rakosi, *Amulet*. NDP234.
Raja Rao, *Kanthapura*. NDP224.
Herbert Read, *The Green Child*. NDP208.
Jesse Reichek, *Etcetera*. NDP196.
Kenneth Rexroth, *Assays*. NDP113.
  An Autobiographical Novel. NDP281.
  Bird in the Bush. NDP80
  Collected Shorter Poems. NDP243.
  100 Poems from the Chinese. NDP192.
  100 Poems from the Japanese.† NDP147.
Charles Reznikoff, *By the Waters of Manhattan*. NDP121.
  Testimony: The United States 1885–1890. NDP200.
Arthur Rimbaud, *Illuminations*.† NDP56.
  Season in Hell & Drunken Boat.† NDP97.

Saikaku Ihara, *The Life of an Amorous Woman*. NDP270.
Jean-Paul Sartre, *Baudelaire*. NDP233.
  Nausea. NDP82.
  The Wall (Intimacy). NDP272.
Delmore Schwartz, *Selected Poems*. NDP241.
Stevie Smith, *Selected Poems*. NDP159.
Gary Snyder, *The Back Country*. NDP249.
  Earth House Hold. NDP267.
Enid Starkie, *Arthur Rimbaud*. NDP254.
Stendhal, *Lucien Leuwen*.
  Book I: *The Green Huntsman*. NDP107.
  Book II: *The Telegraph*. NDP108.
Jules Supervielle, *Selected Writings*.† NDP209.
Dylan Thomas, *Adventures in the Skin Trade*. NDP183.
  A Child's Christmas in Wales. Gift Edition. NDP181.
  Portrait of the Artist as a Young Dog. NDP51.
  Quite Early One Morning. NDP90.
  Under Milk Wood. NDP73.
Lionel Trilling, *E. M. Forster*. NDP189.
Martin Turnell, *Art of French Fiction*. NDP251.
Paul Valéry, *Selected Writings*.† NDP184.
Vernon Watkins, *Selected Poems*. NDP221.
Nathanael West, *Miss Lonelyhearts & Day of the Locust*. NDP125.
George F. Whicher, tr.,
  The Goliard Poets.† NDP206.
J. Willett, *Theatre of Bertolt Brecht*. NDP244.
Tennessee Williams, *Hard Candy*. NDP225.
  The Glass Menagerie. NDP218.
  In the Bar of a Tokyo Hotel & Other Plays. NDP287.
  In the Winter of Cities. NDP154.
  One Arm & Other Stories. NDP237.
  The Roman Spring of Mrs. Stone. NDP271.
  27 Wagons Full of Cotton. NDP217.
William Carlos Williams,
  The William Carlos Williams Reader. NDP282.
  The Autobiography. NDP223.
  The Build-up. NDP259.
  The Farmers' Daughters. NDP106.
  In the American Grain. NDP53.
  In the Money. NDP240.
  Many Loves. NDP191.
  Paterson. Complete. NDP152.
  Pictures from Brueghel. NDP118.
  The Selected Essays. NDP273.
  Selected Poems. NDP131.
  White Mule. NDP226.
John D. Yohannan,
  Joseph and Potiphar's Wife. NDP262.

Complete descriptive catalog available free on request from New Directions, 333 Sixth Avenue, New York 10014.

† Bilingual.